An illustrated introduction
to the main events in Britain,
Ireland and Europe in the late
16th century, the 17th century,
and the early 18th century.

Colourpoint Educational

RIVALRY
and
CONFLICT

Austin Logan

Kathleen Gormley

Illustrated by
John Brogan

Author's note

Austin died on the 19th September 1995 when this book was in its final stages of preparation. It was an honour to work with him "for he was a teacher who walked in the shadows of the temple among his followers and gave not of his wisdom but his faith and his lovingness".

Kahlil Gibran

Special note: The illustrator of this book, John Brogan, wishes his work here to be viewed as a memorial to Austin Logan. Austin saw many of these pictures before he died.

© A. Logan
  K. Gormley   10 9 8 7
  Omagh, 1995

ISBN 10: 1 898392 12 9

ISBN 13: 978 1898392 12 5

Layout and design: Colourpoint Books
Printed by: W & G Baird Ltd

Colourpoint Books
Colourpoint House, Jubilee Business Park
21 Jubilee Road
NEWTOWNARDS
Co Down
BT23 4YH

Tel: (028) 9182 0505
Fax: (028) 9182 1900
E-mail: info@colourpoint.co.uk
Web site: www.colourpoint.co.uk

The Authors

The late Austin Logan gained a BA (Hons) in European and Irish History, an MA in History and Education and a PhD in Approaches to Teaching and Learning. He designed classroom materials, wrote articles on the teaching of history, and was Adviser for Environment and Society with the Western Education and Library Board from 1990 until his untimely death in 1995. He is co-author of *Britain, Ireland and Europe from 1570 to 1745*, published by Colourpoint in 1994. He is also a co-author of the Special Needs text for the compulsory Study Unit 'Union to Partition' to be published in 1996. He was Project Co-ordinator of the cross border working party which has produced a resource for Key Stage 2, *Life in Early Times*, also to be published in 1996.

Kathleen Gormley has a BA (Hons) in Modern History and is currently studying for an MA in History at the University of Ulster. She teaches History and Politics at St Cecilia's Secondary School, Derry. From 1993 - 1995 she was seconded to the Western Education and Library Board as a History Advisory Teacher. She is Past-President of the North-West Archeological and Historical Society, Hon Sec of the Federation for Ulster Local Studies and a member of the Historic Monuments Council for Northern Ireland. She is author of several local history publications and has worked on a variety of educational publications.

Acknowledgments
Pages 11, 14, 34 Scottish National Portrait Gallery
Pages 30, 31 © Crown copyright. Reproduced with the permission of the Controller of HMSO
Pages 33, 58 Tim Webster
Page 42 Nigel Morrison
Page 59 Courtesy of the Director, National Army Museum, London
Pages 60, 61 National Gallery of Ireland
Pages 50, 54, 55 Hulton Deutsch Picture Library

The colours on this page show you the colour of the page you are looking for. For example, the chapter on Charles I and the Puritans is on page 38, and it is a pink page.

Contents

1. The Reformation

This is a picture of Martin Luther preaching.

In 1500 every country in Europe was ruled by Catholic kings and queens.

Then, in 1517, a monk called **Martin Luther** spoke out about the riches of the Catholic Church. He said that some people thought that they could buy their way into Heaven.

The Pope tried to arrest Luther, but he kept on protesting. His followers became known as **Protestants** and the movement he started was the **Reformation**.

Soon Europe was divided into Protestant and Catholic countries. This was to cause much **rivalry** and **conflict** between them for many years to come.

!

Make a list of some of the reasons why Luther complained about the Catholic church.

Key Words: Catholic, Protestant, Reformation, rivalry, conflict.

2. England and Spain 400 years ago

In the sixteenth century, England and Spain were two of the most powerful countries in Europe. England was ruled by **Queen Elizabeth I** from 1558 to 1603 and Spain was ruled by **King Philip II** from 1556 until 1598. Both of them wanted to control, not only their own country, but other countries. Elizabeth was a Protestant and Philip was a Catholic, and as there was tension between Catholics and Protestants in Europe, Elizabeth and Philip became great rivals.

Scotland

England

?

1 Draw or trace the maps showing England and Spain. Colour England in green. Colour Spain in red.

2 How many years did Philip II rule?

3 How many years did Elizabeth rule?

Key Words: rivals, tension.

3. Elizabeth and Philip — rivals

This picture shows a Spanish ambassador presenting Philip II's proposal of marriage to Elizabeth I. She is refusing.

There were other reasons why Elizabeth I and Philip II were rivals. Elizabeth I was a proud woman. She was a daughter of Henry VIII and her family, the **Tudors**, had ruled England since 1485.

Philip II was also a proud king. He came to the throne in 1556 and his father was Emperor Charles V. Philip II was married to Elizabeth's half-sister Mary Tudor.

When she died in 1558, he asked Elizabeth to marry him. Elizabeth said "no" and Philip never forgave her.

In pairs, think of two reasons why Elizabeth refused to marry Philip. Share these with the rest of the class to find out which are the most popular reasons.

Key Words: ambassador, the Tudors, Emperor.

4. Facts about Elizabeth and Philip

ELIZABETH

Born — 1533
Ruled England — 1558 - 1603
   Never married
Religion — Protestant
   Large navy and powerful army
Father — Henry VIII, King of
   England
Wars — defeated Spain in 1588
Died — March 24th 1603

PHILIP

Born — 1527
Ruled Spain — 1556 - 1598
   Four wives. His second wife was
   Mary Tudor, half-sister of
   Elizabeth I
Religion — Catholic
   Large navy
Father — Emperor Charles V
   Lost war against England in 1588
Died — September 13th 1598

The following sentences describe the lives of Elizabeth and Philip. Put them into the order in which they happened:

Elizabeth was born

Philip was born

Elizabeth became Queen

Elizabeth died

Philip became King

Philip died

Philip married Mary Tudor

War between England and Spain

5. Conflict over new lands

Elizabeth and Philip came into conflict over trade and territory.

A country could become rich through trade. Countries bought and sold goods to make money. If a country ruled a lot of territory outside its own borders, it could become rich. It could bring goods from other lands, where it got them cheaply, and then sell them for a profit.

Soon Elizabeth I and Philip II were fighting over new lands that had been discovered in other parts of the world.

One of these new lands was America.

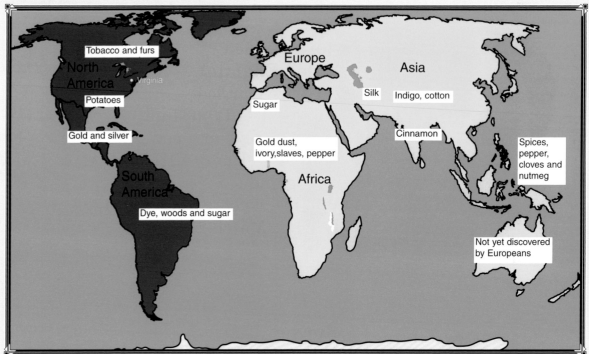

Tobacco and furs

North America

Virginia

Potatoes

Gold and silver

South America

Dye, woods and sugar

Europe

Asia

Silk

Indigo, cotton

Sugar

Gold dust, ivory, slaves, pepper

Cinnamon

Africa

Spices, pepper, cloves and nutmeg

Not yet discovered by Europeans

Look at the map.

1 Which of the following were discovered in America — tobacco, salt, spices, gold, silver, potatoes?

2 Why were these important discoveries?

3 Which ones are important in Ireland today?

?

Key Words: trade, territory, goods, borders, profit.

6. Catholic and Protestant Countries in Europe

Not only were Elizabeth I and Philip II in conflict at this time, but most other countries took sides in the rivalries in Europe.

Protestant countries	Catholic countries
Norway	Portugal
Sweden	Spain
Denmark	France
Switzerland	Ireland
England	Italy
Scotland	

◄————◄— Germany —►————►

Germany is shown across both columns above because there were both Protestants and Catholics there.

These countries helped each other if one of them was in conflict with a country of the other religion.

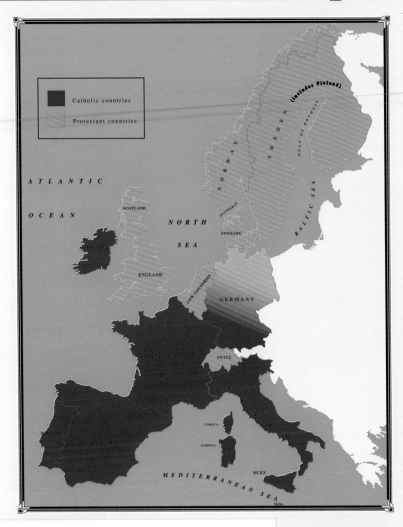

? 1 Name three Catholic countries.

2 Name three Protestant countries.

3 What was the main religion in Ireland at this time?

Work sheet 2

Discuss the following statements about Europe in the sixteenth century and then answer TRUE or FALSE. You might want to put them on cards and make a game.

1. Spain was a Catholic country.

2. Elizabeth I was a Catholic queen.

3. Martin Luther protested against the Catholic church.

4. The Reformation was the start of the Catholic church.

5. Philip II was King of Germany.

6. Mary Tudor was a half sister of Elizabeth I.

7. Trade and territory could make a country rich.

8. Norway was a Catholic country at this time.

9. Italy was a Protestant country.

8. Mary Queen of Scots

One of the most interesting stories of this time was about **Mary Queen of Scots**, who was a cousin of Elizabeth I of England. Mary became Queen of Scotland in 1542 when she was only 6 days old. She was sent to France to be brought up as a Catholic princess. Later she married Francis, heir to the French throne. At 17, Francis' father died and Mary became Queen of France as well as Scotland. In 1560, both her husband and her mother died. Mary was 18 so she came back to Scotland to become queen of that country.

In 1565 she married the **Earl of Darnley** and had a son called James. Mary and her husband did not have a happy marriage and when Darnley was murdered a lot of people thought that Mary had organised it. Shortly after Darnley's death Mary married the Earl of **Bothwell**. The Protestant lords in Scotland did not like Mary because she was a Catholic, so they made her son James, King of Scotland in 1569. Mary fled to England for safety and her cousin Elizabeth allowed her to stay in one of her castles there.

This is a painting of Mary Queen of Scots. Why do you think famous people had their picture painted? Why didn't they just get their photograph taken?

Key Words: heir, organised, fled.

ELIZABETH

Born — 7th September 1533
Died — 24th March 1603
Parents — Henry VIII of England and Anne Boleyn
Appearance — tall, thin, fair complexion, hazel eyes, yellow/red hair, bad teeth.
Other information — Knew Greek and Latin well; intelligent, witty but had a bad temper; spent lots on clothes; had 2000 dresses.

MARY

Born — 8th December 1542
Died — 8th February 1587
Parents — James V of Scotland and Mary of Guise
Appearance — golden-red hair, hazel eyes, tall, thin, described as being very beautiful.
Other information — Well educated, spoke fluent French. Also spoke other languages. Loved animals and wore pearls.

See if these statements are true or false by looking at all the information on this page.

Mary was younger than Elizabeth.

Elizabeth had black hair.

Elizabeth liked clothes.

Mary liked pearls.

Mary did not like dogs.

Elizabeth had blue eyes.

Both queens had kings for fathers.

Mary died before Elizabeth.

Only one could speak foreign languages.

Elizabeth's mother was called Anne.

10. *Mary in England*

Many Catholics in Europe did not want the Protestant Elizabeth I to be ruler in England and they planned to get rid of her and put Mary Queen of Scots in her place. Elizabeth was not sure what to do with Mary.

IF —   she sent her back to Scotland there would be a Catholic ruler in the country beside her.

IF —   she sent her to France, she might attack England later.

IF —   she sent her back to Scotland, the Scots might kill her.

IF —   she executed Mary, Catholic countries might attack her.

IF —   she let Mary stay in England, Catholics might try to make her Queen.

? If you had been Elizabeth, which decision would you have taken about Mary Queen of Scots?

This picture shows Elizabeth trying to make up her mind whether or not to have Mary executed. The death notice lies on the table. Should she sign it?

Key Words: plot, invade, executed.

11. Mary is executed

This is a picture of the execution of Mary Queen of Scots. Why do you think there is a fire burning outside?

Using the painting and the written account, tell the story of the execution of Mary Queen of Scots in your own words.

Key Words: execution, death warrant, corpse.

In 1587 Elizabeth signed Mary's death warrant. Mary's head was chopped off on the 4th February 1587 at Fotheringay Castle.

The following account was written by a man called Robert Wyngfield and called 'A true presentation of the Execution of Mary Queen of Scots':

"With a smiling face she (Mary) turned to her servants standing behind the platform. They were weeping. The Queen bid them farewell.

She knelt down on a cushion and prayed. She laid herself upon the block quietly. It took two strokes of the axe before the executioner cut off her head. Then a little dog was spotted under the dead queen's clothes. It would not leave Mary's body and came and lay at her shoulder."

12. *Studying what really happened in the past*

Sources do not always agree about what happened in the past.

There are two sources on page 14. One is the picture and one is the account written by Robert Wyngfield.

Look carefully at these two sources and see if they agree or disagree with each other.

Do they both tell us that :

> Mary smiled
>
> there was a fire outside
>
> Mary knelt on a cushion
>
> there were lots of people there
>
> Mary was executed with an axe
>
> her dog was there
>
> her servants cried?

1 In your class, were all the accounts of Mary's execution the same?

2 Why do you think sources sometimes disagree with each other?

3 Do you think it is important for an historian to study more than one source about the past? Why?

13. The Spanish Armada 1588

You have already looked at some of the reasons why England and Spain were rivals.

Both countries were rich.

English sailors fought with Spanish sailors over treasure from America.

Look at the panel on the right to see more reasons.

It was no surprise then, that in 1558 a great fleet of ships called **The Armada** set sail from Spain to attack England.

Elizabeth I of England was a powerful Queen.	Philip II of Spain was a powerful King.
Elizabeth I was a Protestant.	Philip II was a Catholic.
Elizabeth I executed Mary, Queen of Scots, a Catholic Queen, in 1587.	Philip II was married to Mary Tudor, Elizabeth's half sister. When she died in 1558 Philip thought he should be King of England.
Elizabeth helped people who did not like Philip.	Philip II asked Elizabeth I to marry him but she refused.

!

Elizabeth I and Philip II went to war for personal reasons, power reasons and money reasons. Give an example of each reason.

Right: Some of the Armada ships get ready to sail.

16

14. Timeline — 1588

1   20 May .... 130 Armada ships set sail from different ports.

2   19 June .... The Armada stops in Corunna for food. The weather is stormy.

3   19 July .... The English spot the Armada coming. They light fires along the coast of Cornwall.

4   21 July .... English ships fight the Armada in the English Channel.

5   27 July .... The Armada stops in Calais.

6   29 July .... The English drive the Armada to the north.

7   Aug/Sept ...... 20 Armada ships are sunk as they sail around the coast of Scotland to escape the English.

8   September ... 24 Armada ships are sunk as they sail around the west coast of Ireland trying to get home.

9   Sept/Oct .... The rest of the Armada ships arrive in Santander full of sick and starving men.

15. The Armada sets sail from Spain

!

Trace the map on this page.

Look at the timeline on page 17. Each statement has a number beside it.

Mark the numbers on your map where you think they should be. Number 1 is already done for you.

Now join the numbers together in the right order.

Now you have drawn the route that the Armada took.

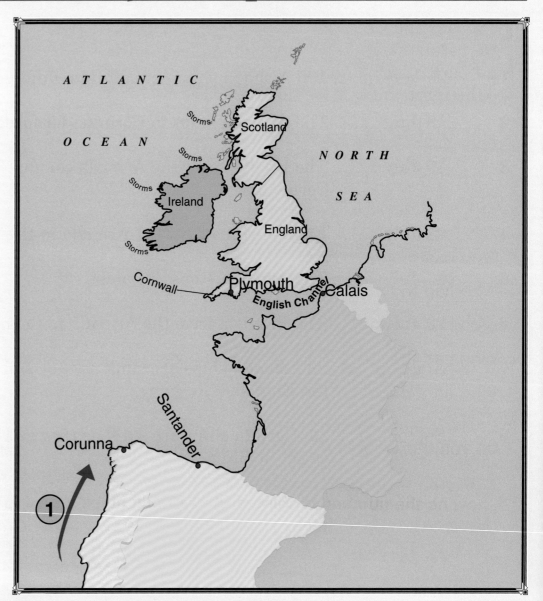

16. The English and Spanish ships

Spain and England had built up their fleets because they had been planning war with each other.
On the right you can see the size of the two fleets.

?

Who had the most ships?   How many?

Who had the most sailors?   How many?

Who had the most soldiers?   How many?

Who had the most cannon?   How many?

Who fired the most shots?   How many?

Looking at the answers to these questions, who do you think would win the battle? Why?

With your teacher's help, draw a bar graph showing the number of ships and cannon that England and Spain had. Use red for Spain and green for England.

	Spain		England
	130	ships	102
	8,050	sailors	14,385
	18,973	soldiers	1,540
	1,124	cannon	1,972
	19,369	lbs of shot fired	14,677

Key Words: fleets, cannon.

17. *The Great Armada is defeated*

The great Spanish Armada lost the battle with the English, and many ships were wrecked as they fled for home. Spain had lost the war and Elizabeth I was a hero. But for the ordinary sailor the war at sea had been terrible.

?

1 What can you see in the picture?

2 What would you hear if you were there?

3 What do you think the Spanish sailors are thinking?

4 What would you smell if you were there?

5 What do you think happens next?

This picture shows some sailors on board one of the Spanish ships.

18. What is a colony?

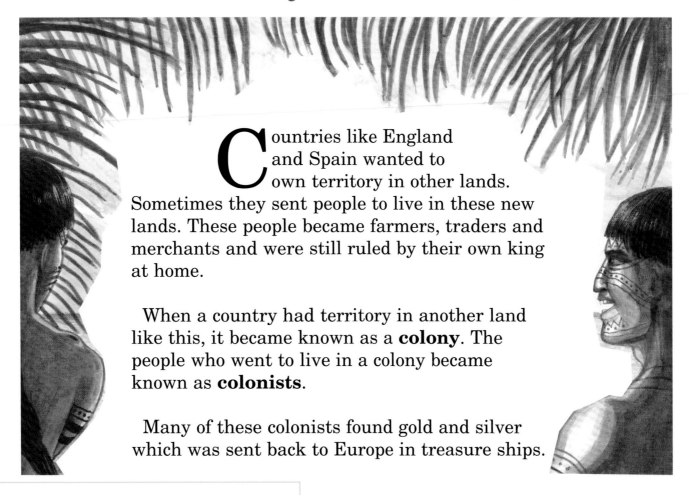

Countries like England and Spain wanted to own territory in other lands. Sometimes they sent people to live in these new lands. These people became farmers, traders and merchants and were still ruled by their own king at home.

When a country had territory in another land like this, it became known as a **colony**. The people who went to live in a colony became known as **colonists**.

Many of these colonists found gold and silver which was sent back to Europe in treasure ships.

 List some of the things which were found in the new colonies.

Key Words: merchants, colony, colonists, territory.

19. Fact or Fantasy?

In the 15th and 16th century Spain and Portugal started colonies in many parts of the world, especially South America. Explorers returned from South America with stories of many strange sights, some of which were true and some of which were not.

The picture above shows some of the real things which the colonists in South America said they saw.

The picture on the right shows some of the creatures which they said they saw.

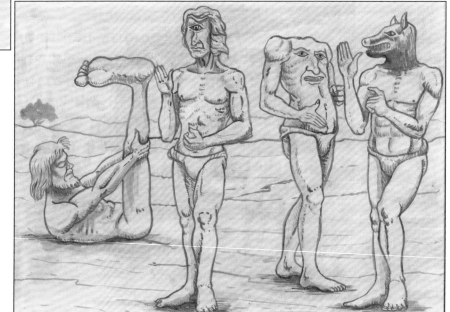

20. The first colonists in America

The first colonists arrived in America, (also called the **New World**) with **Christopher Columbus** in **1492**. When they arrived on the island of Hispaniola there were one million Arawak Indians. After fifty years, the entire Indian population had either been worked to death, been killed, or died from diseases such as smallpox, malaria, measles and influenza.

Many thousands of native Americans committed suicide.

1 What do you think Columbus thought of the native people? Think of words like useful, sick, stupid, slaves.

2 What do you think the native people thought of Columbus? Think of words like cruel, threatening, kind, strange.

3 Why would they think these things about each other?

This picture shows Columbus coming ashore in America for the first time.

When he first saw the Indians he wrote in his diary:

"They are completely defenceless and have no skill at arms — and so they are fit to be ordered about and do anything else that is needed".

Key Words: disease, suicide.

21. An English colony in America

Some of the first people to leave England went to a colony in America, called Jamestown. The sentences on the right tell their story. The sentences are not in the right order. Write them out again in the right order.

1 The colonists sailed in 3 ships for America.

7 Soon, the Indians were beaten by the better weapons of the colonists.

4 Then they built houses for themselves.

5 They planted vegetables and made nets for catching food in the forest and rivers.

6 At first they fought with the Indians.

2 They reached Chesapeake Bay in April 1607.

8 Then they traded with the Indians.

3 The colonists chose a site and built a fort so that they would be safe.

This picture shows the first settlers arriving on the beach in America and meeting the Indians for the first time. Why is there a box on the ground and what do you think the white men are saying to the Indians?

Key Words: Indians, site.

22. Ireland 400 years ago

At this time, Ireland was a Catholic country and was ruled by Elizabeth I of England. Many Irish chiefs wanted to rule their own territory. They took part in a war against Elizabeth I, which lasted for nine years from 1594 until 1603.

The Irish chiefs were led by **Hugh O'Neill**, but they were defeated at the Battle of Kinsale in 1601.

Elizabeth I wanted to keep control of Ireland and to make the Irish people obedient to her rule.

Sir George Carew was an official of Elizabeth I's in Ireland. He said:

"We must change Irish government, clothing, customs, manner of holding land, language and habits of life to make them obedient."

Key Words: chief, obedient, government.

?

1 The picture above shows an Irish chief with his army. What do you think is happening in the picture?

2 What would these Irish people think of what Sir George Carew said?

23. The Plantation of Ireland

Elizabeth I decided that one of the best ways to keep Ireland obedient was to give land in Ireland to English and Scottish people, who would then live there and keep the country in control. She wished to 'plant' Ireland and make it a colony.

This became known as **plantation**. The people who came to Ireland were known as **planters**. They were Protestants and would be loyal to the English crown. Many native Irish people, who were Catholics, were against this.

Who do you think would make the following statements, Elizabeth I or an Irish chieftain?

1 I want to be a Catholic.

2 I want everyone in Ireland to speak English.

3 This country must first be broken by war.

4 I want to speak Gaelic.

5 I want to be ruled by Irish laws.

6 I want Ireland to obey English law.

7 The best way to control Ireland is by plantation.

24. The Planters come to Ireland

Elizabeth I carried out a plantation in Ireland in 1586. This was known as the Munster Plantation. It included such places as Limerick, Waterford, Cork and Kinsale.

An earlier plantation had taken place in 1556 in Laois and Offaly.

However the biggest plantation of all took place in Ulster, in 1609, when James I was the king.

Ulster was the part of Ireland which was most against the English throne. Land in places such as Donegal, Londonderry, Tyrone, Fermanagh, Cavan and Armagh were given by the government to many English and Scottish people.

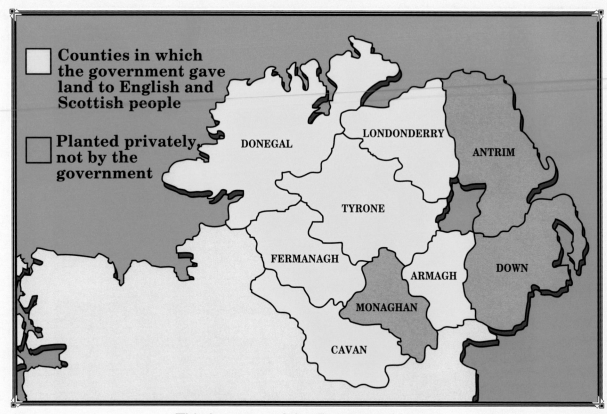

Counties in which the government gave land to English and Scottish people

Planted privately, not by the government

This is a map of the Province of Ulster

Trace the map of Ulster on this page.

!

1   How many counties are in the province of Ulster?

2   On your tracing, shade in and label the counties where the government gave land to English and Scottish planters.

25. The Flight of the Earls 1607

One of the main reasons why James I was able to 'plant' Ulster successfully was that the main Ulster chieftains had fled from Ireland in 1607. This event was known as **The Flight of the Earls**.

The leader of the Ulster chieftains was Hugh O'Neill, who had been beaten by the English on Christmas Eve 1601, at the Battle of Kinsale in Co Cork.

After the defeat at Kinsale, the English strengthened their forts in Ulster, and finally in 1607, O'Neill decided that the only choice left to him was to leave for Spain.

The picture on this page shows the Flight of the Earls. The Earls left Ireland from Rathmullan. Can you find Rathmullan on a map?

What do you think O'Neill was thinking as he left Ireland for Spain? You could mention

* the defeat at Kinsale

* leaving from Rathmullan

* his last words to people on the shore

26. The Ulster Plantation

James I sent Protestant Scottish and English settlers as part of the **Ulster Plantation**. Four million acres of land were given to these planters.

The native Irish were put off the land and the planters were to rule the country for England. These planters lived mainly in fortified villages and towns.

Plantation towns and villages which survive to this day include Coleraine, Omagh, Londonderry, Bellaghy, Ballykelly, Moneymore, Magherafelt, Eglinton, Draperstown, Newtownstewart, Enniskillen.

Some towns were named after trades and some were set up by London Companies or **Guilds**. These Companies protected the rights of different trades, eg: grocers, haberdashers, fishmongers, drapers.

These are the shields of two guilds — a Grocers' and a Fishmongers'. Can you tell which is which?

?

1 What is a — grocer, haberdasher, fishmonger, draper?

2 The Grocers' Company used to be called Pepperers'. Why do you think pepper and spices were so important in those days?

3 Design a shield for a London Company.

Key Word: fortified.

27. A Plantation Bawn

attic

flanker

turret

musket loop

bawn wall

gate

Large houses, surrounded by walls, had to be built to protect the new settlers from attacks by native Irish. These houses were known as plantation **bawns**.

The picture on this page shows a drawing of one which was built at Monea in County Fermanagh.

The native Irish who attacked the settlers were called **woodkerne**.

A messenger arrives with news that a group of woodkerne are heading for your village. What do you do?

Key Words: bawn, settlers, woodkerne.

Plantation towns or villages were built to protect the new settlers.

The map shows some of the settlements which were built near Londonderry, by London merchants or guilds, such as Muff (Eglinton) built by the Grocers; Ballykelly, built by the Fishmongers, and Brackfield, built by the Skinners.

Look at the map.

Can you point out all the places and companies mentioned in the text above?

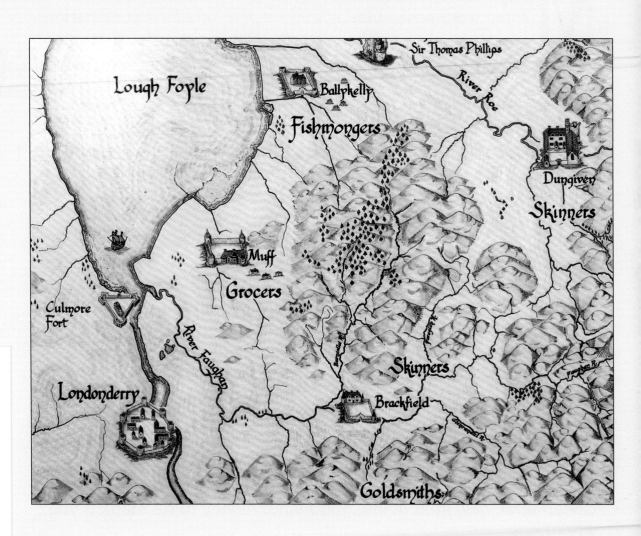

29. Life as a Planter in Ireland

Many different people became planters. Some were rich, some were poor, some were escaping religious persecution and some were on the run from the law. All these people had been promised a better life in Ulster.

For some, this was true, but for others, this was not so.

The native Irish did not like them and there were attacks made on them.

Imagine you are a planter. Write a letter to your relatives in England or Scotland telling them about your life in Ulster. Tell them of some of the good things and some of the bad things about being a planter.

Bad things about being a planter

Bad weather, wolves, hostile Irish rebels, Irish didn't like planters.

Good things about being a planter

Cheap land, new start in life, good land, money to be made if you work hard.

A man called George Canning said: "There is nothing but constant trouble in these parts. Men cannot go near the woods without being in great danger — the Irish went into an Englishman's house. They severely wounded the man of the house and took between £7 and £8 and any of the rest of his goods which were worth carrying away".

Key Words: persecution.

30. *Life as a native Irish person*

Most of the native Irish were not loyal to the English Crown. Many of them lost their lands during the plantation and were forced onto poorer land or else became bandits, living in the hills and woods and attacking the planters.

The O'Cahan clan in North Derry lost most of their castles during the plantation. They were given poor land on the outskirts of Limavady and their last chieftain, Donnell Ballagh, died as a prisoner in the Tower of London.

This is a drawing of a tomb of an O'Cahan chieftain called Cooey-na-Gael which means 'The Terror of the Stranger'.

Read the lines of the poem by Alice Milligan

1 List three things that the O'Cahan's lost because of the Plantation.

2 Which of the following words do you think that the O'Cahans might use about the people who took their land — thieves, friends, enemies, kind people, murderers, good neighbours.

Explain why you picked these words.

"There is not one acre left to him, nor to any Lord of his line.
No house at Enagh, or Faughan Vale, no cattle in Glenconkeine"

from a poem by Alice Milligan, called *The Rapparee*.

31. James I becomes King 1603-1625

When Elizabeth I died in 1603, **James I**, the son of Mary Queen of Scots, became the King of England and Scotland. James was Scottish and a Protestant. He believed that God has given him the right to rule England and that Parliament should obey him. This was called the **Divine Right of Kings**. Parliament did not agree with this and so a quarrel began, which was to end in the **English Civil War**.

!

Discuss with your teacher the meaning of 'divine right' and 'civil war'.

The picture on this page is a portrait of King James I of England.

Key Words: **Parliament, divine right.**

32. King and Parliament

Not only was there a lot of rivalry and conflict between the countries of Europe, but in England there was also rivalry and conflict between the King and Parliament. This led to a **civil war** and to the execution of the King.

One of the reasons for this conflict was that the King thought he was sent by God to rule England. This was known as having a **'divine right'** to rule.

Key Words: **civil war.**

!

Match these words to their correct meanings:

civil war   when the state kills a person for crimes

divine right   war between two sets of people in the same country

execution   the crowned ruler of a country

parliament   given power by God to be king

king   people elected to rule

Describe this picture. What do you think the different parts of it mean?

33. *Charles I, King of England 1625-1649*

When James I died in 1625 his son **Charles I** became king. Charles also thought that he was a King appointed by God and that his word was law. Parliament did not think that they should be ruled by a twenty-five year old King and refused to give him enough money to run the country. When he was refused money by Parliament, Charles I tried to arrest five Members of Parliament but they escaped.

Here is Charles I trying to arrest five members of Parliament.

Key Words: throne, taxes

?

Who would agree with these statements — Parliament or the King?

Parliament should be the partner of the King.

Kings are chosen by God to rule.

The King is not to be trusted.

The King should rule the country alone.

Parliament should not give the King money if they disagree with what he is doing.

34. Kings and Parliament in the 17th century

Eleven of the words below are hidden in the wordsquare. Find them and write them out.

EXECUTED
PEOPLE
PARLIAMENT
POWERFUL
QUEEN
KING
VOTE
TAXES
COMMONS
COUNTRY
OBEY
GOVERNMENT
MINISTER
POWER
LAW

A	C	P	X	D	C	O	M	M	O	N	S
P	Z	A	O	N	A	Q	U	E	E	N	A
X	D	R	D	D	M	L	M	N	Q	Y	C
T	Y	L	L	X	P	C	I	L	Y	A	K
A	T	I	U	A	P	B	N	E	L	A	W
X	A	A	Y	C	E	G	I	M	V	K	P
E	M	M	V	O	T	E	S	S	H	I	O
S	E	E	A	C	S	H	T	B	G	N	W
Y	S	N	N	O	U	T	E	E	D	G	E
L	I	T	M	L	M	L	R	S	A	C	R
T	L	T	O	E	X	E	C	U	T	E	D
G	O	V	E	R	N	M	E	N	T	T	S

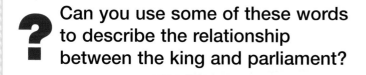

? Can you use some of these words to describe the relationship between the king and parliament?

Key Words: law, government, commons, minister, vote

35. Charles I and the Puritans

Charles I had religious problems with the Scots because he tried to force them to use the Church of England prayer-book. This led to a war in 1638 which the Scots won.

There was another group who did not like the King either, because their religious beliefs were different to his. They were called **Puritans**. They had very strict rules of their own and they wanted these rules to become the law of the land. The king would not agree to this.

Oliver Cromwell was a Puritan.

?

1 What religion was Oliver Cromwell?

2 Which of the Puritan laws would you find hardest to keep?

3 Would you like to have laws like this today?

Puritan laws were very strict.

In 1650, there was a law which tried to stop women wearing make-up.

Here are some other things which could happen —

- If you mended a dress on a Sunday, you could be put in the stocks

- If you walked as far as the next village on a Sunday, you could be fined 50p

- Teenage boys who played football on a Sunday were whipped

You will find out more about the Puritans on pages 43 and 44

36. The English Civil War begins in 1642

Royalists were sometimes called Cavaliers. This is what a Cavalier looked like. The Cavaliers supported the king during the Civil War.

The Civil War started in April **1642**. The supporters of the King were known as **Royalists** or **Cavaliers**. The supporters of Parliament were known as **Roundheads**. The King's forces started well. The nobles and country squires were good horse-soldiers and many nobles brought men from their estates to fight for the King. By 1643, the Royalists were advancing on London, which was held by the Roundheads.

Parliament was worried, but a Puritan general, called **Oliver Cromwell**, came to their rescue, with his well-trained troops, the **Ironsides**.

The Scots also sent an army to help the Roundheads.

This is what a Roundhead looked like. The Roundheads supported Parliament and Cromwell during the Civil War.

Key Words: Cavalier, Roundhead, horse-soldier

37. *Two important battles*

There were two major battles fought in the English Civil War. In 1644 the Scots advanced across the border and joined the Roundhead army. Prince Rupert, who was the leader of the Royalists, was taken by surprise.

This picture shows what one of these big battles would have looked like. Would you have liked to fight in a battle like this?

THE BATTLE OF MARSTON MOOR

On 2nd July 1644, as the Royalist army were busy cooking their supper, the Roundheads made a surprise attack at **Marston Moor** and scattered them. The Roundheads had won the first major battle of the Civil War.

THE BATTLE OF NASEBY

In 1645, Oliver Cromwell and his Ironsides destroyed the King's army at **Naseby**. In June 1646 the Royalist headquarters at Oxford was captured. After this Charles gave himself up to the Scots.

38. Defeat and execution for Charles I, 1649

After Charles was defeated he was brought to trial by Parliament. He was found guilty and sentenced to die.

On 30th January 1649, Charles I was executed in Whitehall, London. It was a cold day and Charles wore two shirts so that people would not think that he was shivering with fear. He wanted to die as he had ruled England — a proud man. Great crowds gathered to watch the execution. As he was about to have his head cut off, the crowd fell silent. Many were glad that he was about to die and many were sad; but all could not believe that such a king was about to die before their eyes. He climbed up to the scaffold and in the silent air the crowd could hear the swish of the mighty axe as it came down upon his thin neck, with a sickening thud of metal on skin and bone.

His head was chopped from his body and a gush of blood ran red across the scaffold. The crowd gasped in amazement and horror as the king's body shook for one last time, and then lay still. His head lay severed with his eyes still open.

You are a reporter at this execution. Write the story for your newspaper. You may wish to use a computer to help you.

Key Word: scaffold.

39. *Parliament rules England, 1649-1660*

With Charles I dead, England was ruled by Parliament. This time was known as the **Commonwealth**, when England was without a King from **1649 until 1660**. The House of Lords was done away with and bishops were sacked. Each church was run by a minister and an elected committee.

These **Puritans** were strict. Nearly all kinds of entertainment were banned and other religions were put down.

The picture on the left shows what the inside of a Church of England church looked like.

The picture on the right shows what the inside of a Puritan church looked like.

List the differences between the two churches.

40. The Puritans

Oliver Cromwell was a religious man and he made rules which were very strict. He believed that religion should be simple and that churches should be plain. People should dress modestly and live quietly. People who followed this religion were called **Puritans**. 'Puritan' was a nickname for those people who wanted to purify the church. If someone was found mending a dress or going for a walk on a Sunday they could be put into the stocks.

Some Puritan rules were:
THOU SHALT NOT
* dance
* wear make-up
* work or wash clothes on Sunday
* travel on Sunday except to church
* eat on feast days
* wear fancy clothes
* go to fancy churches

Make a list of the laws you agree or disagree with.

Here a Puritan man and woman are on their way to church.

Key Words: modestly, nickname, the stocks

41. The Puritan family

The father was the head of the Puritan family. He was master of the house and his word was law. Puritan children addressed him as 'Sir'. Puritans believed children were bad but could be saved by a good upbringing.

Parents gave their children unusual names, such as Zeal of the Hand, Obadiah, or Praise be God Barebones. Popular children's names were: Faith, Patience, Ruth, Hope, Joshua, Abraham or Joseph.

Many of these names came from the Bible.

This picture shows a Puritan family praying and listening to readings from the Bible.

?

Find two of the names mentioned above in the Bible. Can you think of two more which the Puritans might have used?

42. The 1641 Rebellion

In the year 1641 there was a bloody revolution in Ireland, particularly in Ulster. Ulster Catholics had lost their lands to the English and Scottish planters during the Ulster Plantation and they were unhappy about this. They decided to use violence to change the situation. 10,000 - 15,000 Protestants were massacred in this rebellion. There was a cruel incident at Portadown, Co Armagh in November 1641.

Later, a Scottish general, called Munro, took revenge by massacring many rebel Catholics at Loughbrickland, Co Down.

A

The historian Robert Kee wrote a book in 1980 called *Ireland, A History*. In it he wrote:

On a cold November day in 1641 ... some 100 Protestant men, women and children, who had been seized from their homes, robbed and stripped of most of their clothes, were hoarded together onto the bridge at Portadown. They were thrown or driven over the parapet into the water below, where they were drowned, or if they could swim, were shot or knocked on the head as they came ashore.

This picture was drawn about 1645. We do not know if the artist was there, or whether he drew this after hearing about it. On the left, Robert Kee describes the same incident in his modern book.

Key Words: rebellion, parapet

43. The 1641 Rebellion in Co Armagh

A man called William Clarke managed to escape, and he told his story later. On the right, he is describing *his* experience of the same incident you read about on page 45.

On pages 45 and 46 you will see three sources. They are labelled A, B, and C.

1 Look at the illustration of the massacre in Portadown, Source B. Can you see: 100 Protestant people
      stripped settlers
      bridge
      people being thrown into the water
      people being shot or knocked on the head?

2 Copy out those you can see in Source B on a table like the one started below. Look at Sources A and C. If they also have this information tick the box.

Source A	Source B	Source
√	bridge	√

C

This is William Clarke's story. Remember, he was actually there:

'We were locked up, 100 men and children in Loughgall church. Many were sore, tortured by strangling and half hanging... then driven like hogs six miles to the River Bann in Portadown ... pushed onto the bridge, stripped naked and then forced by pikes into the river... those that did not drown were shot at by the rebels as they tried to swim ashore ... I was saved by paying a rebel £15. The leader of the rebels was Toole McCann.'

44. The story of Jane Armstrong

Here is Jane Armstrong telling her story.

The 1641 rebellion started on the night of 23rd October. Here is a story told by Jane Armstrong on 3rd May 1653 when she was aged about 16 or 17.

'I was living in the town of Lissan (Tyrone) at the start of the rebellion in 1641, with my grandfather Andrew Young, who kept an inn. One evening James McIveagh came in with the others to drink for about two or three hours, and then they all left again. But within an hour McIveagh came back again when Andrew Young was in bed. He called for him to rise and drink with him — McIveagh drank with him, but then began to pick a quarrel with him about a falling out that he had had with Andrew Young's son. Soon McIveagh drew a sword from his cloak and stuck it in Andrew Young's side. Andrew Young died two or three hours later without speaking a word. McIveagh left this house as soon as he had committed this murder'.

?

1 What age was Jane Armstrong in 1641?

2 What did her grandfather do for a living?

3 Would James McIveagh have been drunk on the evening of the murder? How do you know?

4 Do you believe Jane Armstrong's version of the story?

5 If you knew that James McIveagh was a Catholic and Andrew Young was a Protestant, would it change your view of what happened?

6 Tell in your own words what happened.

45. War in Ireland, 1641–1650

In July 1642 Owen Roe O'Neill arrived in Ulster with troops and money from Europe to help the Ulster Catholics.

In October 1645 O'Neill, and in June 1646 the Ulster rebels, defeated the Scots army at Benburb in Co Armagh and killed half of them.

O'Neill's army was not strong enough to attack Dublin and the English parliament sent more troops to Ireland.

In August 1649, 12,000 soldiers of Oliver Cromwell's **New Model Army** arrived. This army was an army which had been formed from Cromwell's **Ironsides**, which are mentioned on page 39. He captured the towns of Drogheda, Wexford, New Ross, Cork, Youghal, Bandon, Kinsale, Kilkenny and Clonmel.

When Cromwell left Ireland in 1650 the rebels were well and truly beaten.

 Make a short timeline of events in Ireland from 1641 – 1650.

46. "To Hell or Connaught"

As a reward for defeating the Irish, Cromwell gave Irish land to many of his soldiers, to pay them for fighting for him. As a result, many Irish people lost their land. Even those who were allowed to keep property were given smaller and poorer farms in the west of Ireland.

The land in the western province, known as **Connaught**, was very poor. Many Irish people thought it was like Hell and many used the slogan **"To Hell or Connaught"**.

By 1655 all Catholic landowners had left their lands and moved to a tougher life in Connaught.

Cromwell also made life difficult for Catholic priests. About 1000 priests were forced out of Ireland during the 1650s. After a few years some of them began to return to say mass and preach in secret.

What does "To Hell or Connaught" mean?

This picture shows Oliver Cromwell dressed for battle.

47. *Oliver Cromwell — Lord Protector*

After capturing Drogheda, Cromwell said:

"When the troops surrendered, their officers were knocked on the head, and every tenth soldier was killed. .... I think that this is a good punishment from God for Irish rebels who have their hands stained in blood.'

Oliver Cromwell was the most powerful man in England in the middle of the seventeenth century. He was born in 1599 and his family were farmers. He was a large man with plain tastes. He had a strong belief in God and thought that God had a job for him to do.

He often showed that he was a brave soldier and later an excellent commander. He was also a great believer in Parliament and was against the **Divine Right of Kings**.

He led the Parliament side in the Civil War which started in 1642. (Go back to pages 39 and 40 to remind yourself about this). His own troops, or **Ironsides**, became an important part of his **New Model Army** which won victories in the Civil War at Naseby, Dunbar and Worcester. In 1653 he took the title **Lord Protector of the Commonwealth**.

When he came to Ireland, Cromwell was ruthless against the rebel Irish.

Cromwell died in 1658 and when Charles II became king, Cromwell's body was dug up and hanged at Tyburn. Nevertheless Cromwell should be remembered as a brilliant soldier.

48. England gets a king again

When Oliver Cromwell died in 1658, Parliament had lost its strong leader. There was no-one to replace him. Charles I had a son who was also called Charles. When he promised to rule England with the help of Parliament, it was decided to allow him back to the throne of England.

He was called **Charles II**. So kings were now brought back as rulers and this was known as the **Restoration**. Some of the people who had signed the death warrant of Charles I, were now themselves condemned to death by hanging, drawing and quartering.

From 1660 onwards England was never to be without a king or queen again.

This picture shows what death by hanging, drawing and quartering was. Can you work it out? Who do you think the two men in armour are?

Key Words: Restoration, drawing, quartering.

49. James II becomes King of England in 1685

The king in the picture above is Charles II. Can you find out who the monarchs on the right are? You should be able to find out from looking at the rest of this book.

Charles II ruled England from 1660-1685. During this time there were more arguments between the King and Parliament. Parliament tried to pass a law to stop Charles' brother **James** from becoming King and Charles dismissed them.

Parliament said he was just like his father Charles I, and there were plots against him.

By the time Charles' brother became James II in 1685, England was as divided as ever and James was unpopular. He was also a Catholic.

In 1688, Parliament asked James' daughter Mary and her husband William of Orange, who were both Protestants, to become King and Queen of England.

50. The Glorious Revolution, 1688

William of Orange, landed in England on 5th November **1688**, with a large army. James II escaped quietly to France by taking a boat down the River Thames. Parliament asked William III and his wife Mary II to be their Protestant king and queen.

Parliament wanted to make sure that future rulers would not be

* No Catholic could become king.
* Catholics could not vote.
* Only Parliament could decide on laws and taxes.
* Parliament controlled the army.

The days of Divine Right of Kings were over. This was known as **The Glorious Revolution**.

? Why do you think Parliament brought in these laws?

Catholics and they also wanted to make sure that Catholics would not become powerful. Over the next few decades they passed new laws and they also reminded the king of old ones.

Some of these laws are beside the picture below.

This picture shows King William landing in England in 1688.

Key Word: decades.

53

51. Rulers during the war in Ireland 1689 - 1692

Ireland was still ruled by England at this time, and many battles between James II and William III were fought there.

Ireland was still a Catholic country so James II, a Catholic, hoped to get support from the French King Louis XIV, who was also a Catholic.

The main rulers at this time

Louis XIV

Louis XIV (1638-1715)

77 years old when he died
King of France
Wanted power for himself
Catholic
Took himself seriously
Worked very hard
Wanted France to rule Europe
Had 17 children, many lovers
Had a poor sense of humour

William III (1650-1702)

52 years old when he died
King of Netherlands, England, Ireland
Brilliant general
Spent his life fighting the French
Clever, hard worker, ruthless
Could speak 6 languages
Suffered from asthma, hump back
Always worked late at night
Fell from his horse and died

William III

James II

James II (1633-1701)

68 years old when he died
King of England
Catholic
Slow, dull, no sense of humour
Very poor general
Very strict ruler
Had at least 3 children
Lost the throne of England
Lost the Siege of Derry
Lost the Battle of the Boyne
Fled to France

Mary II (1662-1694)

32 years old when she died
Queen of England
Wife of William III
Protestant
Lived in Holland for 12 years
Had no children
Got married aged 15
Died of smallpox
Ruled England jointly with
William
Strong in her views
Good to friends and forgiving to
enemies
Was admired by her armies

Mary II

52. *The main battles in Ireland*

There were four main battles in Ireland between James II and William III

* the Siege of Derry, 1689

* the Battle of the Boyne, 1690

* the Battle of Aughrim, July 1691

* the Siege of Limerick, August - September 1691

53. *The Siege of Derry , 1689*

In March 1689 James II landed at Kinsale in Ireland with 400 French officers, and arms and ammunition for 10,000 men. This army was known as the **Jacobite** army and was made up of Englishmen, Frenchmen and Irishmen.

At first, all went well for the Jacobites. All of Ireland, except for Ulster, was controlled by them and panic spread to Ulster Protestants. Thousands fled, and many went to the walled cities of Londonderry and Enniskillen.

James' army then marched towards Londonderry and camped outside the gates in April 1689.

In a famous incident, thirteen apprentice boys had already closed the gates against the Jacobites in December 1688.

This is a picture showing the scene when the apprentice boys closed the gates of Derry in 1688. What do you think some of the people are shouting?

Key Words: Jacobite, apprentice.

57

More about the Siege of Derry 1689

This is a picture of what the scene in Derry might have looked like when the Mountjoy arrived. What do you think the people of the city were most anxious to unload from this ship? Who do you think the people on the hill in the background are?

James II demanded that Derry surrender. The Governor was called Lundy and he opened negotiations with James.

However, the citizens of the city called Lundy a traitor and got rid of him.

Derry was surrounded by a mile of high, thick walls, and as James' army hadn't the guns to batter down the walls, he tried to starve the city for 105 days.

The Jacobite army built a barrier across the river to stop food getting in, but on 30th July 1689, a ship called the **Mountjoy** broke through at Culmore, and the city was saved.

54. The Battle of the Boyne, July 1690

In March 1690, 7,000 French troops came to help James, but King William himself landed at Carrickfergus, and marched to Dundalk.

James II moved from Dublin to meet him and on 1st July **1690**, the two armies met at the River **Boyne** in Co Meath. King William's army crossed the river first and the army of King James began to panic. The Jacobites were outnumbered by three to one and only the Jacobite cavalry fought well.

At the end of the first day, James had fled south and left in a ship for France, where the news of his defeat at the Boyne was greeted with annoyance by Louis XIV.

However elsewhere in Europe there was rejoicing.

This painting of The Battle of the Boyne is by a Dutch artist called Jan Wyck.

Key Words: *outnumbered, cavalry.*

55. The Battle of Aughrim, July 1691

This is a painting of the Jacobite leader, Patrick Sarsfield.

The Jacobite army was also at Aughrim, blocking the Williamite's way to Galway. **Patrick Sarsfield**, a Jacobite leader, suggested that the Jacobite army withdraw to Limerick but **St Ruth**, the French commander of the Jacobites, decided to fight.

The Jacobites fought well for a few hours until St Ruth was killed and they were scattered. In July 1691, Galway surrendered. One of William's commanders was called **General Ginkel**. He marched on Limerick, which eventually surrendered.

A treaty was finally signed in October 1691.

Key Word: treaty.

56. The Siege of Limerick, August-September 1691

The remains of James' army went westwards after the Battle of Aughrim, to defend Limerick and Athlone.

They were quickly followed by William, who laid siege to the City of Limerick, which was also surrounded by strong walls. The Jacobite soldiers at Limerick were led by Patrick Sarsfield who managed to destroy a great quantity of William's guns at Ballyneety.

However, William still attacked Limerick in August 1690, but could not capture the city. As heavy autumn rains came in, William gave up and left Ireland. He left General Ginkel in charge and Ginkel tried to make peace with the Jacobites.

Eventually peace was made and the **Treaty of Limeric**k was signed.

This is a painting of the Williamite commander, General Ginkel, painted by Sir Godfrey Kneller in 1695

57. *The Treaty of Limerick, 1692*

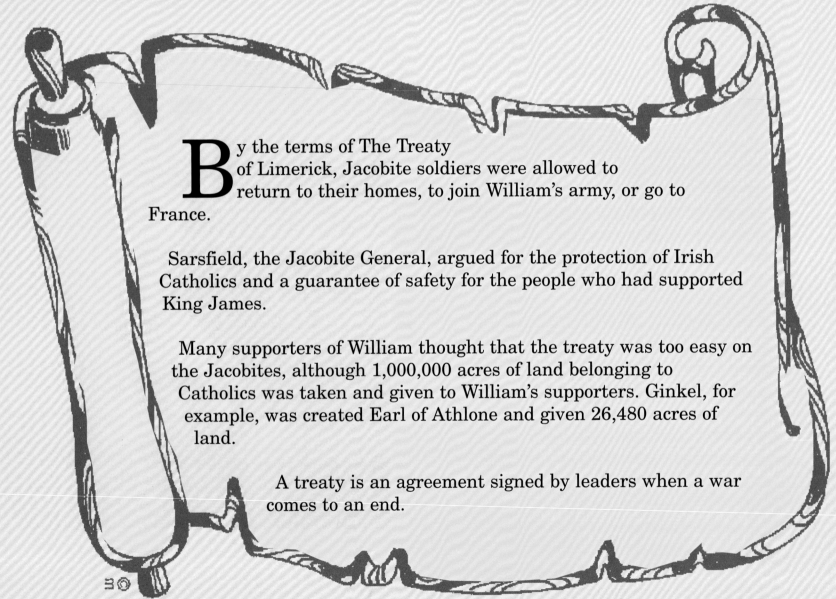

By the terms of The Treaty of Limerick, Jacobite soldiers were allowed to return to their homes, to join William's army, or go to France.

Sarsfield, the Jacobite General, argued for the protection of Irish Catholics and a guarantee of safety for the people who had supported King James.

Many supporters of William thought that the treaty was too easy on the Jacobites, although 1,000,000 acres of land belonging to Catholics was taken and given to William's supporters. Ginkel, for example, was created Earl of Athlone and given 26,480 acres of land.

A treaty is an agreement signed by leaders when a war comes to an end.

58. The Wild Geese

As a result of The Treaty of Limerick, 11,000 Jacobite soldiers left Ireland in ships provided by General Ginkel. Most of these soldiers entered the army of Louis XIV. They remained loyal to James and his son, James III.

For the rest of the 18th century, thousands of Irishmen, called the **The Wild Geese**, left Ireland to join this brigade and other brigades in the Catholic armies of Europe.

Many laws were passed to make sure that control in Ireland remained in the hands of the Protestants. They were afraid of Catholics and did not want them to have any power in Ireland.

These laws were known as the **Penal Laws** and they were made by the parliament in Dublin.

They prevented Catholics from having a say in the running of the country.

It was only after 1780 that many of these laws disappeared.

Who were the Wild Geese? Why do you think they were called this?

Timeline

1517   Martin Luther complained about the Catholic church

1553   Mary Tudor became Queen of England

1556   Philip II became King of Spain

1558   Mary Tudor died. Her sister Elizabeth became Queen of England

1569   Mary Queen of Scots fled to England

1586   The first plantation of Ireland by Elizabeth I

1587   Mary Queen of Scots was executed

1588   The Spanish Armada

1594   Elizabeth's war with Hugh O'Neill. It lasted nine years

1601   The Battle of Kinsale

1603   Elizabeth I died. James I became King

1607   The Flight of the Earls
Colonists arrived in Jamestown

1609   James I sent planters to Ulster

1625   James I died. Charles I became King

1641   Rebellion in Ireland

1642   Civil War in England

1649   Charles I executed. England became a Commonwealth with no king

1660   The King restored to the throne. Charles II became King

1685   Charles II died and James II became King

1688   The Glorious Revolution. William and Mary became King and Queen

1689   The Siege of Derry

1690   The Battle of the Boyne

1691   The Battle of Aughrim

1692   The Siege and Treaty of Limerick